45 Apple Recipes for Home

By: Kelly Johnson

Table of Contents

- Classic Apple Pie
- Caramel Apple Crisp
- Baked Apple Dumplings
- Apple Cider Donuts
- Apple Fritters
- Homemade Applesauce
- Apple and Cheddar Stuffed Chicken
- Waldorf Salad
- Apple Cinnamon Pancakes
- Apple and Brie Quesadillas
- Apple Cider Sangria
- Apple Butter
- Apple and Walnut Salad
- Apple and Cinnamon Muffins
- Apple Slaw
- Apple and Sage Pork Chops
- Apple and Cranberry Stuffed Acorn Squash
- Apple Galette
- Apple and Cinnamon Oatmeal
- Apple and Gouda Grilled Cheese
- Apple and Almond Smoothie
- Apple and Sausage Stuffed Mushrooms
- Apple and Cinnamon Pull-Apart Bread
- Apple and Caramelized Onion Pizza
- Apple and Cranberry Baked Brie
- Apple and Cinnamon Scones
- Apple and Pecan Stuffed Pork Tenderloin
- Apple and Goat Cheese Crostini
- Apple and Cranberry Chutney
- Apple and Cinnamon Granola
- Apple and Cider Glazed Chicken
- Apple and Thyme Roasted Turkey
- Apple and Cinnamon Energy Balls
- Apple and Rosemary Roasted Vegetables
- Apple and Cranberry Quinoa Salad

- Apple and Cinnamon French Toast
- Apple and Walnut Chicken Salad
- Apple and Caramel Bread Pudding
- Apple and Cinnamon Popcorn
- Apple and Cheddar Soup
- Apple and Cinnamon Rice Pudding
- Apple and Cranberry Stuffed Pork Chops
- Apple and Pomegranate Guacamole
- Apple and Cinnamon Rice Krispie Treats
- Apple and Cheddar Hand Pies

Classic Apple Pie

Ingredients:

For the Pie Crust:

- 2 1/2 cups all-purpose flour
- 1 cup unsalted butter, cold and diced
- 1 teaspoon salt
- 1 teaspoon sugar
- 1/4 to 1/2 cup ice water

For the Apple Filling:

- 6 cups peeled, cored, and thinly sliced apples (such as Granny Smith or a mix of varieties)
- 3/4 cup granulated sugar
- 1/4 cup light brown sugar, packed
- 1 tablespoon lemon juice
- 1 teaspoon ground cinnamon
- 1/4 teaspoon ground nutmeg
- 1/4 teaspoon salt
- 3 tablespoons cornstarch or all-purpose flour (to thicken)

For Assembly:

- 1 tablespoon butter, cut into small pieces (for dotting on top)
- 1 egg, beaten (for egg wash)
- 1 tablespoon sugar (for sprinkling on top)

Instructions:

For the Pie Crust:

Prepare the Dough:
- In a food processor, pulse together the flour, salt, and sugar. Add cold, diced butter and pulse until the mixture resembles coarse crumbs.
- Gradually add ice water, one tablespoon at a time, and pulse until the dough starts to come together. Avoid adding too much water.

- Divide the dough in half, shape each half into a disc, wrap in plastic wrap, and refrigerate for at least 1 hour.

Roll Out the Crust:
- Preheat your oven to 375°F (190°C).
- On a lightly floured surface, roll out one disc of dough to fit a 9-inch pie dish. Place the rolled-out crust into the dish and trim any excess.

For the Apple Filling:

Prepare the Apples:
- In a large bowl, combine sliced apples with lemon juice to prevent browning.
- In a separate bowl, mix together granulated sugar, brown sugar, cinnamon, nutmeg, salt, and cornstarch.
- Toss the sliced apples with the sugar and spice mixture until evenly coated.

Assembly and Baking:

Fill the Pie:
- Pour the apple filling into the prepared pie crust, mounding the apples slightly in the center.
- Dot the top of the apples with small pieces of butter.

Roll Out the Top Crust:
- Roll out the second disc of dough and place it over the apples. Trim and crimp the edges to seal the pie.

Ventilation and Egg Wash:
- Cut a few slits on the top crust to allow steam to escape during baking.
- Brush the top crust with the beaten egg and sprinkle with sugar for a golden finish.

Bake:
- Place the pie on a baking sheet to catch any drips. Bake in the preheated oven for 45-55 minutes or until the crust is golden brown and the filling is bubbling.

Cool and Serve:
- Allow the pie to cool for a few hours before slicing. Serve with a scoop of vanilla ice cream if desired.

This classic apple pie recipe yields a deliciously flaky crust and a spiced apple filling that captures the essence of this timeless dessert. Enjoy!

Caramel Apple Crisp

Ingredients:

For the Apple Filling:

- 6 cups peeled, cored, and sliced apples (such as Granny Smith or a mix of varieties)
- 1/2 cup granulated sugar
- 1/4 cup light brown sugar, packed
- 1 tablespoon all-purpose flour
- 1 teaspoon ground cinnamon
- 1/4 teaspoon ground nutmeg
- 1/4 teaspoon salt
- 1 tablespoon lemon juice

For the Caramel Sauce:

- 1/2 cup unsalted butter
- 1 cup light brown sugar, packed
- 1/4 cup heavy cream
- 1 teaspoon vanilla extract
- Pinch of salt

For the Crisp Topping:

- 1 cup old-fashioned oats
- 1/2 cup all-purpose flour
- 1/2 cup light brown sugar, packed
- 1/4 cup chopped pecans or walnuts (optional)
- 1/2 cup unsalted butter, melted

Instructions:

Preheat the Oven:
- Preheat your oven to 350°F (175°C).

Prepare the Apple Filling:

- In a large bowl, combine the sliced apples with granulated sugar, brown sugar, flour, cinnamon, nutmeg, salt, and lemon juice. Toss until the apples are well coated.

Make the Caramel Sauce:
- In a saucepan over medium heat, melt the butter. Add brown sugar, heavy cream, vanilla extract, and a pinch of salt. Stir continuously until the sugar is dissolved and the mixture is smooth. Remove from heat.

Combine Apples and Caramel:
- Pour a portion of the caramel sauce over the apple mixture, reserving some for serving. Toss the apples until evenly coated with the caramel.

Transfer to Baking Dish:
- Transfer the caramel-coated apples to a greased 9x13-inch baking dish or a similar-sized oven-safe dish.

Prepare the Crisp Topping:
- In a separate bowl, combine oats, flour, brown sugar, and chopped nuts if using. Pour melted butter over the dry ingredients and mix until crumbly.

Assemble and Bake:
- Sprinkle the crisp topping evenly over the caramel-coated apples.
- Bake in the preheated oven for 40-45 minutes or until the topping is golden brown, and the apples are tender.

Serve:
- Allow the caramel apple crisp to cool for a few minutes before serving.

Drizzle with Caramel Sauce:
- Drizzle the remaining caramel sauce over the crisp just before serving.

Enjoy:
- Serve warm, optionally with a scoop of vanilla ice cream or a dollop of whipped cream.

This Caramel Apple Crisp offers a perfect blend of sweet and tart apples, a gooey caramel layer, and a crunchy oat topping. It's a comforting and indulgent dessert, especially enjoyable during the fall season. Enjoy!

Baked Apple Dumplings

Ingredients:

For the Apple Dumplings:

- 6 medium-sized baking apples (such as Granny Smith)
- 1 package refrigerated crescent roll dough (8 rolls)
- 1/2 cup unsalted butter, melted
- 1 cup granulated sugar
- 1 teaspoon ground cinnamon
- 1/2 teaspoon vanilla extract
- 1/2 cup chopped nuts (pecans or walnuts), optional

For the Syrup:

- 1 cup water
- 1/2 cup granulated sugar
- 1/2 teaspoon ground cinnamon
- 1/4 cup unsalted butter

Instructions:

Preheat the Oven:
- Preheat your oven to 350°F (175°C).

Prepare the Apples:
- Peel and core the apples. Cut each apple into 8 wedges.

Roll the Dumplings:
- Unroll the crescent roll dough and separate it into triangles. Place an apple wedge on the wide end of each triangle.
- In a small bowl, mix together sugar, cinnamon, vanilla extract, and melted butter. Brush each apple wedge with the sugar and cinnamon mixture. If desired, sprinkle chopped nuts over the apples.

Wrap the Apples:
- Roll each apple wedge in the crescent roll dough, starting from the wide end. Place the wrapped dumplings in a greased baking dish with the pointed ends facing down.

Prepare the Syrup:
- In a saucepan, combine water, sugar, cinnamon, and butter. Bring the mixture to a boil, stirring until the sugar is dissolved. Remove from heat.

Pour Syrup Over Dumplings:
- Pour the hot syrup over the apple dumplings in the baking dish.

Bake:
- Bake in the preheated oven for 35-40 minutes or until the dumplings are golden brown and the apples are tender.

Serve:
- Serve the baked apple dumplings warm, spooning some of the syrup over each serving.

Optional Garnish:
- Garnish with a sprinkle of cinnamon or a scoop of vanilla ice cream if desired.

Enjoy:
- Enjoy these delightful baked apple dumplings as a delicious and comforting dessert!

These baked apple dumplings are a delightful treat with a flaky, golden crust and tender, cinnamon-spiced apples. The syrup adds a sweet and buttery finish to this classic dessert. Enjoy!

Apple Cider Donuts

Ingredients:

For the Donuts:

- 2 cups apple cider
- 2 cups all-purpose flour
- 1/2 cup whole wheat flour
- 2 teaspoons baking powder
- 1/2 teaspoon baking soda
- 1/2 teaspoon salt
- 1 teaspoon ground cinnamon
- 1/4 teaspoon ground nutmeg
- 1/4 teaspoon ground allspice
- 1/4 cup unsalted butter, melted
- 1/2 cup granulated sugar
- 1/2 cup brown sugar, packed
- 2 large eggs
- 1 teaspoon vanilla extract

For the Cinnamon Sugar Coating:

- 1/2 cup granulated sugar
- 1 teaspoon ground cinnamon
- 1/4 cup unsalted butter, melted

Instructions:

Reduce Apple Cider:
- In a saucepan, simmer the apple cider over medium heat until it is reduced to 1 cup. Allow it to cool.

Preheat the Oven:
- Preheat your oven to 375°F (190°C). Grease a donut pan.

Prepare Dry Ingredients:
- In a bowl, whisk together the all-purpose flour, whole wheat flour, baking powder, baking soda, salt, cinnamon, nutmeg, and allspice.

Mix Wet Ingredients:

- In another bowl, whisk together the melted butter, granulated sugar, brown sugar, eggs, and vanilla extract. Add the reduced apple cider and mix until well combined.

Combine Wet and Dry Ingredients:
- Add the wet ingredients to the dry ingredients and stir until just combined. Do not overmix.

Fill the Donut Pan:
- Spoon the batter into a piping bag or a zip-top bag with a corner snipped off. Pipe the batter into the greased donut pan, filling each cavity about two-thirds full.

Bake:
- Bake in the preheated oven for 12-15 minutes or until a toothpick inserted into a donut comes out clean.

Prepare Cinnamon Sugar Coating:
- In a bowl, mix together granulated sugar and ground cinnamon.

Coat the Donuts:
- While the donuts are still warm, dip each one into the melted butter and then roll in the cinnamon sugar mixture to coat.

Serve and Enjoy:
- Serve the apple cider donuts warm and enjoy the delicious, spiced flavor!

These Apple Cider Donuts are a delightful fall treat, combining the flavors of apple cider and warm spices. The cinnamon sugar coating adds a sweet and slightly crunchy finish. Enjoy!

Apple Fritters

Ingredients:

For the Fritters:

- 2 cups all-purpose flour
- 1/3 cup granulated sugar
- 1 teaspoon baking powder
- 1/2 teaspoon baking soda
- 1/2 teaspoon salt
- 1 teaspoon ground cinnamon
- 2/3 cup buttermilk
- 2 large eggs
- 1 teaspoon vanilla extract
- 2 cups apples, peeled, cored, and finely chopped (such as Granny Smith)
- Vegetable oil for frying

For the Glaze:

- 2 cups powdered sugar
- 1/4 cup milk
- 1 teaspoon vanilla extract

Instructions:

For the Fritters:

Prepare the Dry Ingredients:
- In a large bowl, whisk together the flour, sugar, baking powder, baking soda, salt, and cinnamon.

Mix the Wet Ingredients:
- In another bowl, whisk together the buttermilk, eggs, and vanilla extract.

Combine Wet and Dry Ingredients:
- Pour the wet ingredients into the dry ingredients and stir until just combined. Do not overmix.

Add Chopped Apples:

- Gently fold in the chopped apples, ensuring they are evenly distributed throughout the batter.

Heat Oil for Frying:
- In a deep, heavy-bottomed pan or a deep fryer, heat vegetable oil to 350°F (175°C).

Drop Spoonfuls into Hot Oil:
- Using a spoon or a cookie scoop, carefully drop spoonfuls of batter into the hot oil. Fry until golden brown, flipping halfway through for even cooking. This may take about 3-4 minutes per side.

Drain on Paper Towels:
- Once golden brown, use a slotted spoon to remove the fritters from the oil and place them on a plate lined with paper towels to drain excess oil.

For the Glaze:

Make the Glaze:
- In a bowl, whisk together powdered sugar, milk, and vanilla extract until smooth.

Dip Fritters in Glaze:
- While the fritters are still warm, dip each one into the glaze, coating it evenly.

Serve and Enjoy:
- Allow the glaze to set for a few minutes, and then serve the apple fritters warm.

These Apple Fritters are a delightful treat, with a crispy exterior, a tender inside, and a sweet glaze that adds the perfect finish. Enjoy these delicious fritters as a breakfast treat or a tasty snack!

Homemade Applesauce

Ingredients:

- 6-8 apples (a mix of sweet and tart varieties like Granny Smith and Gala works well)
- 1/2 cup water
- 1/4 cup granulated sugar (adjust to taste)
- 1 teaspoon ground cinnamon
- 1 tablespoon lemon juice (optional, to prevent browning)

Instructions:

Prepare the Apples:
- Peel, core, and chop the apples into chunks. If you prefer chunky applesauce, cut the apples into larger pieces. For smoother applesauce, chop them into smaller pieces.

Cook the Apples:
- In a large saucepan, combine the chopped apples, water, sugar, and ground cinnamon.
- Cook over medium heat, stirring occasionally, until the apples are tender and easily mashed with a fork. This usually takes about 15-20 minutes.

Mash the Apples:
- Once the apples are soft, use a potato masher or the back of a spoon to mash them to your desired consistency. For a smoother applesauce, you can use a blender or food processor.

Adjust Sweetness:
- Taste the applesauce and adjust the sweetness if needed. Add more sugar if you prefer a sweeter applesauce.

Add Lemon Juice (Optional):
- If you want to prevent browning and add a bit of brightness, stir in lemon juice.

Cool and Serve:
- Allow the applesauce to cool before serving. You can serve it warm or chilled, depending on your preference.

Store:
- Store the homemade applesauce in an airtight container in the refrigerator. It can be kept for several days.

Additional Tips:

- Experiment with different apple varieties to find the flavor profile you enjoy the most.
- Adjust the cinnamon and sugar quantities according to your taste preferences.
- Feel free to add a pinch of nutmeg or cloves for extra spice.

Homemade applesauce is a versatile and delicious treat. Enjoy it on its own, as a topping for pancakes or yogurt, or use it as a substitute in recipes that call for applesauce.

Apple and Cheddar Stuffed Chicken

Ingredients:

For the Chicken:

- 4 boneless, skinless chicken breasts
- Salt and black pepper to taste
- 1 tablespoon olive oil

For the Apple and Cheddar Stuffing:

- 1 cup finely chopped apples (such as Granny Smith)
- 1 cup shredded sharp cheddar cheese
- 1/4 cup chopped pecans or walnuts
- 1/4 cup dried cranberries (optional)
- 1/2 teaspoon ground cinnamon
- Salt and black pepper to taste

For the Pan Sauce:

- 1 tablespoon butter
- 1 tablespoon all-purpose flour
- 1 cup chicken broth
- Salt and black pepper to taste

Instructions:

Prepare the Stuffing:

Mix Ingredients:
- In a bowl, combine chopped apples, shredded cheddar cheese, chopped nuts, dried cranberries (if using), ground cinnamon, salt, and black pepper. Mix well.

Prepare the Chicken:

Preheat Oven:
- Preheat your oven to 375°F (190°C).

Butterfly the Chicken:
- Lay each chicken breast flat on a cutting board. With a sharp knife, cut horizontally through the thickest part of the breast, almost but not quite through, to create a pocket.

Season and Stuff the Chicken:
- Season the inside of each chicken breast with salt and black pepper. Stuff each pocket with the apple and cheddar mixture.

Secure with Toothpicks:
- Secure the openings with toothpicks to hold the stuffing in place.

Sear the Chicken:
- In an oven-safe skillet, heat olive oil over medium-high heat. Sear the stuffed chicken breasts for 2-3 minutes on each side until golden brown.

Bake:
- Transfer the skillet to the preheated oven and bake for about 20-25 minutes or until the chicken is cooked through.

Prepare the Pan Sauce:

Make a Roux:
- In the same skillet, melt butter over medium heat. Add flour and whisk to create a roux.

Add Chicken Broth:
- Gradually whisk in chicken broth, stirring constantly to avoid lumps. Bring the mixture to a simmer.

Season:
- Season the sauce with salt and black pepper to taste.

Serve:
- Remove toothpicks from the chicken breasts. Serve the stuffed chicken with the pan sauce drizzled over the top.

Enjoy your Apple and Cheddar Stuffed Chicken, a delicious combination of savory chicken with sweet and tangy apple and sharp cheddar flavors!

Waldorf Salad

Ingredients:

For the Salad:

- 2 cups diced apples (such as Granny Smith or a mix of sweet and tart varieties)
- 1 cup diced celery
- 1 cup seedless red grapes, halved
- 1/2 cup chopped walnuts
- 1/2 cup raisins or dried cranberries (optional)
- Fresh lettuce leaves for serving

For the Dressing:

- 1/2 cup mayonnaise
- 2 tablespoons Greek yogurt or sour cream
- 1 tablespoon lemon juice
- 1 tablespoon honey
- Salt and black pepper to taste

Instructions:

Prepare the Salad Ingredients:
- In a large mixing bowl, combine diced apples, diced celery, halved grapes, chopped walnuts, and raisins or dried cranberries (if using). Toss the ingredients together.

Prepare the Dressing:
- In a separate bowl, whisk together mayonnaise, Greek yogurt or sour cream, lemon juice, honey, salt, and black pepper. Adjust the sweetness and acidity to your taste.

Combine Dressing with Salad:
- Pour the dressing over the salad and gently toss until all ingredients are well coated.

Chill:
- Cover the bowl and refrigerate the Waldorf Salad for at least 30 minutes to allow the flavors to meld.

Serve:

- When ready to serve, line a serving dish or individual plates with fresh lettuce leaves. Spoon the Waldorf Salad onto the lettuce.

Garnish (Optional):

- Optionally, garnish with a sprinkle of additional chopped walnuts or a drizzle of honey on top.

Enjoy:

- Serve and enjoy your refreshing and crunchy Waldorf Salad!

Feel free to customize this Waldorf Salad to your liking by adjusting the types of apples, nuts, or other ingredients. It's a versatile and timeless salad that's perfect for a light lunch, side dish, or as a refreshing addition to a picnic.

Apple Cinnamon Pancakes

Ingredients:

For the Pancakes:

- 1 cup all-purpose flour
- 2 tablespoons granulated sugar
- 1 teaspoon baking powder
- 1/2 teaspoon baking soda
- 1/4 teaspoon salt
- 1 teaspoon ground cinnamon
- 3/4 cup buttermilk
- 1/4 cup milk
- 1 large egg
- 2 tablespoons unsalted butter, melted
- 1 teaspoon vanilla extract
- 1 cup finely chopped apples (such as Granny Smith)

For Topping:

- Sliced apples
- Maple syrup
- Whipped cream (optional)
- Chopped nuts (optional)

Instructions:

Prepare the Dry Ingredients:
- In a large mixing bowl, whisk together flour, sugar, baking powder, baking soda, salt, and ground cinnamon.

Prepare the Wet Ingredients:
- In another bowl, whisk together buttermilk, milk, egg, melted butter, and vanilla extract.

Combine Wet and Dry Ingredients:
- Pour the wet ingredients into the dry ingredients and stir until just combined. Do not overmix; lumps are okay.

Add Chopped Apples:
- Gently fold in the chopped apples into the pancake batter.

Preheat Griddle or Pan:
- Preheat a griddle or a non-stick pan over medium heat. Lightly grease with cooking spray or butter.

Cook Pancakes:
- Scoop 1/4 cup portions of batter onto the griddle for each pancake. Cook until bubbles form on the surface, then flip and cook until golden brown on the other side.

Keep Warm:
- Keep cooked pancakes warm in a low oven while you cook the remaining batter.

Serve:
- Stack the pancakes on a plate, top with sliced apples, a drizzle of maple syrup, and any optional toppings like whipped cream or chopped nuts.

Enjoy:
- Serve immediately and enjoy these delicious Apple Cinnamon Pancakes!

These pancakes are perfect for a cozy breakfast or brunch, especially during the fall season. The combination of sweet apples and warm cinnamon makes them a comforting and flavorful treat.

Apple and Brie Quesadillas

Ingredients:

- 4 large flour tortillas
- 2 medium-sized apples (such as Granny Smith), thinly sliced
- 8 ounces Brie cheese, thinly sliced
- 1/4 cup chopped walnuts or pecans
- 1 tablespoon honey
- 1/2 teaspoon ground cinnamon
- Butter or cooking spray for grilling

Instructions:

Prepare the Ingredients:
- Thinly slice the apples and Brie cheese.

Assemble the Quesadillas:
- Lay out four tortillas. On one half of each tortilla, place a layer of Brie cheese slices, followed by a layer of thinly sliced apples, and a sprinkle of chopped nuts.

Drizzle with Honey and Sprinkle Cinnamon:
- Drizzle honey over the apple slices and sprinkle a pinch of ground cinnamon on top.

Fold and Press:
- Fold the tortillas in half over the filling, creating a half-moon shape. Press down gently to help the ingredients stick together.

Cook on the Stovetop:
- Heat a skillet or griddle over medium heat. Add a small amount of butter or use cooking spray.
- Place the quesadillas on the skillet and cook for 2-3 minutes on each side or until the tortillas are golden brown and the cheese is melted.

Slice and Serve:
- Remove the quesadillas from the skillet and let them cool for a minute. Slice each quesadilla into wedges.

Serve Warm:
- Serve the Apple and Brie Quesadillas warm, optionally with a side of extra honey for dipping.

These quesadillas combine the sweetness of apples, the creamy richness of Brie, and the crunch of nuts for a delightful flavor and texture combination. They make a perfect appetizer, snack, or even a unique lunch option!

Apple Cider Sangria

Ingredients:

- 1 bottle of white wine (750ml), chilled (such as Sauvignon Blanc or Pinot Grigio)
- 2 cups apple cider
- 1/2 cup brandy
- 1/4 cup orange liqueur (like Triple Sec or Cointreau)
- 2 apples, cored and sliced
- 1 orange, thinly sliced
- 1 cinnamon stick
- 1 star anise (optional)
- 1-2 tablespoons honey or maple syrup (adjust to taste)
- Sparkling water or club soda (optional, for serving)
- Ice cubes

Instructions:

Prepare the Fruits:
- Core and slice the apples. Thinly slice the orange.

Combine Ingredients:
- In a large pitcher, combine the chilled white wine, apple cider, brandy, orange liqueur, sliced apples, sliced oranges, cinnamon stick, and star anise (if using).

Sweeten with Honey or Maple Syrup:
- Add 1-2 tablespoons of honey or maple syrup to the pitcher, adjusting the sweetness to your liking. Stir well to combine.

Chill:
- Place the pitcher in the refrigerator and let the sangria chill for at least 2-4 hours, allowing the flavors to meld.

Serve:
- Before serving, give the sangria a gentle stir. You can serve it over ice cubes if desired.

Optional Sparkling Water:
- For a bit of fizz, top off each glass with a splash of sparkling water or club soda.

Garnish:
- Garnish individual glasses with additional apple slices, orange slices, or a cinnamon stick if desired.

Enjoy Responsibly:
- Serve and enjoy your refreshing Apple Cider Sangria responsibly!

This Apple Cider Sangria is perfect for autumn gatherings, parties, or cozy evenings. The combination of crisp white wine, apple cider, and autumn spices creates a delightful and festive drink.

Apple Butter

Ingredients:

- 5-6 pounds of apples (a mix of sweet and tart varieties), peeled, cored, and chopped
- 1 cup granulated sugar
- 1 cup light brown sugar, packed
- 1 tablespoon ground cinnamon
- 1/2 teaspoon ground nutmeg
- 1/4 teaspoon ground cloves
- Pinch of salt
- 1 tablespoon vanilla extract (optional)
- Juice of one lemon

Instructions:

Prepare the Apples:
- Peel, core, and chop the apples into small chunks.

Cook the Apples:
- In a large slow cooker or heavy-bottomed pot, combine the chopped apples, sugars, cinnamon, nutmeg, cloves, salt, and lemon juice. Stir well to coat the apples.

Cook Slow and Low:
- If using a slow cooker, cook on low for about 8-10 hours or until the apples are very soft and can be easily mashed with a fork. If using a pot on the stove, simmer over low heat for 2-3 hours, stirring occasionally.

Blend or Mash:
- Once the apples are soft, you can use an immersion blender to puree the mixture directly in the slow cooker or transfer the mixture to a blender or food processor in batches. Blend until smooth.

Thicken:
- Return the pureed mixture to the slow cooker or pot and continue cooking, uncovered, on low until the apple butter thickens to your desired consistency. This may take an additional 2-3 hours.

Add Vanilla (Optional):
- If using vanilla extract, stir it into the apple butter during the last hour of cooking.

Test for Thickness:

- To test the thickness, place a spoonful of apple butter on a cold plate. If it holds its shape, it's ready.

Cool and Store:
- Allow the apple butter to cool completely. Transfer it to sterilized jars and store in the refrigerator. It can also be frozen in small batches for longer storage.

Enjoy:
- Spread the delicious homemade apple butter on toast, use it as a topping for pancakes or waffles, or incorporate it into various recipes.

Homemade apple butter is a delightful treat, and making it at home allows you to control the sweetness and spice levels to suit your taste preferences. Enjoy!

Apple and Walnut Salad

Ingredients:

For the Salad:

- 4 cups mixed salad greens (lettuce, arugula, spinach, etc.)
- 2 medium apples, thinly sliced (use a mix of sweet and tart varieties)
- 1/2 cup chopped toasted walnuts
- 1/2 cup crumbled feta or goat cheese
- 1/4 cup dried cranberries or raisins (optional)

For the Dressing:

- 3 tablespoons extra-virgin olive oil
- 2 tablespoons apple cider vinegar
- 1 tablespoon honey
- 1 teaspoon Dijon mustard
- Salt and black pepper to taste

Instructions:

Prepare the Salad:

Wash and Dry Greens:
- Wash and thoroughly dry the mixed salad greens.

Slice Apples:
- Thinly slice the apples. If you're preparing the salad in advance, you can toss the apple slices with a bit of lemon juice to prevent browning.

Toast Walnuts:
- In a dry skillet over medium heat, toast the chopped walnuts for a few minutes until they become fragrant. Stir frequently to avoid burning. Remove from heat and let them cool.

Assemble the Salad:
- In a large salad bowl, combine the mixed greens, sliced apples, toasted walnuts, crumbled feta or goat cheese, and dried cranberries or raisins if using.

Prepare the Dressing:

Whisk the Dressing:
- In a small bowl, whisk together the extra-virgin olive oil, apple cider vinegar, honey, Dijon mustard, salt, and black pepper until well combined.

Dress the Salad:
- Drizzle the dressing over the salad just before serving.

Toss Gently:
- Toss the salad gently to ensure all ingredients are coated with the dressing.

Serve:
- Serve the Apple and Walnut Salad immediately as a refreshing and flavorful side dish.

This Apple and Walnut Salad combines the sweetness of apples, the crunch of toasted walnuts, and the tanginess of feta or goat cheese for a delightful flavor and texture combination. Enjoy it as a light lunch or a side dish for dinner!

Apple and Cinnamon Muffins

Ingredients:

- 2 cups all-purpose flour
- 1 1/2 teaspoons baking powder
- 1/2 teaspoon baking soda
- 1/2 teaspoon salt
- 1 teaspoon ground cinnamon
- 1/2 cup unsalted butter, softened
- 1/2 cup granulated sugar
- 1/2 cup brown sugar, packed
- 2 large eggs
- 1 teaspoon vanilla extract
- 1/2 cup buttermilk
- 2 cups peeled, cored, and diced apples (such as Granny Smith)

For the Cinnamon Sugar Topping:

- 2 tablespoons granulated sugar
- 1/2 teaspoon ground cinnamon

Instructions:

Preheat Oven:
- Preheat your oven to 375°F (190°C). Line a muffin tin with paper liners or grease it lightly.

Prepare Dry Ingredients:
- In a bowl, whisk together the flour, baking powder, baking soda, salt, and ground cinnamon. Set aside.

Cream Butter and Sugars:
- In a separate large bowl, cream together the softened butter, granulated sugar, and brown sugar until light and fluffy.

Add Eggs and Vanilla:
- Add the eggs one at a time, beating well after each addition. Stir in the vanilla extract.

Alternate Dry Ingredients and Buttermilk:

- Gradually add the dry ingredients to the wet ingredients, alternating with the buttermilk. Begin and end with the dry ingredients. Mix until just combined.

Fold in Apples:
- Gently fold in the diced apples until evenly distributed in the batter.

Fill Muffin Cups:
- Divide the batter evenly among the muffin cups, filling each about 2/3 full.

Prepare Cinnamon Sugar Topping:
- In a small bowl, mix together the granulated sugar and ground cinnamon for the topping.

Top with Cinnamon Sugar:
- Sprinkle the cinnamon sugar mixture over the tops of each muffin.

Bake:
- Bake in the preheated oven for 18-20 minutes or until a toothpick inserted into the center of a muffin comes out clean.

Cool:
- Allow the muffins to cool in the tin for a few minutes before transferring them to a wire rack to cool completely.

Enjoy:
- Enjoy your delicious homemade Apple and Cinnamon Muffins!

These muffins are perfect for a cozy breakfast or snack, and the combination of apples and cinnamon is a classic and comforting flavor.

Apple Slaw

Ingredients:

For the Slaw:

- 4 cups thinly sliced green cabbage
- 2 cups thinly sliced red cabbage
- 2 large apples, julienned or grated (use a mix of sweet and tart varieties)
- 1 cup shredded carrots
- 1/2 cup chopped fresh cilantro or parsley (optional, for garnish)

For the Dressing:

- 1/3 cup mayonnaise
- 2 tablespoons apple cider vinegar
- 1 tablespoon honey
- 1 teaspoon Dijon mustard
- Salt and black pepper to taste

Instructions:

Prepare the Slaw Ingredients:
- In a large bowl, combine the thinly sliced green and red cabbage, julienned or grated apples, shredded carrots, and chopped cilantro or parsley (if using).

Prepare the Dressing:
- In a separate small bowl, whisk together the mayonnaise, apple cider vinegar, honey, Dijon mustard, salt, and black pepper until well combined.

Combine Slaw and Dressing:
- Pour the dressing over the slaw ingredients and toss until everything is well coated with the dressing.

Chill:
- Cover the bowl and refrigerate the apple slaw for at least 30 minutes to allow the flavors to meld and the slaw to chill.

Garnish (Optional):
- Before serving, garnish with additional chopped cilantro or parsley if desired.

Serve:

- Serve the apple slaw as a refreshing side dish alongside your favorite main courses.

This Apple Slaw is crisp, colorful, and combines the natural sweetness of apples with the crunch of cabbage and carrots. It's a perfect side dish for barbecues, picnics, or as a refreshing addition to any meal.

Apple and Sage Pork Chops

Ingredients:

- 4 bone-in pork chops
- Salt and black pepper, to taste
- 2 tablespoons olive oil
- 2 medium apples, cored and sliced (use a mix of sweet and tart varieties)
- 1 onion, thinly sliced
- 2 cloves garlic, minced
- 1/2 cup chicken broth
- 1/2 cup apple cider or apple juice
- 1 teaspoon Dijon mustard
- 1 teaspoon chopped fresh sage (or 1/2 teaspoon dried sage)
- 1/2 cup heavy cream
- Fresh sage leaves for garnish (optional)

Instructions:

Season and Sear Pork Chops:
- Season pork chops with salt and black pepper on both sides. In a large skillet, heat olive oil over medium-high heat. Sear the pork chops until golden brown on each side, about 3-4 minutes per side. Remove the chops from the skillet and set aside.

Saute Apples and Onions:
- In the same skillet, add sliced apples and onions. Saute until they start to soften and caramelize, about 3-4 minutes.

Add Garlic and Sage:
- Stir in minced garlic and chopped sage, cooking for another minute until fragrant.

Deglaze the Pan:
- Pour in chicken broth and apple cider, scraping the bottom of the skillet to deglaze and incorporate the flavorful bits.

Simmer and Add Mustard:
- Bring the liquid to a simmer. Stir in Dijon mustard and let it cook for a couple of minutes to meld the flavors.

Return Pork Chops:

- Return the seared pork chops to the skillet, nestling them into the apple and onion mixture.

Finish Cooking:
- Cover the skillet and let the pork chops simmer in the apple mixture for about 10-15 minutes or until the internal temperature of the pork reaches 145°F (63°C).

Add Cream:
- Stir in the heavy cream and let it simmer for an additional 2-3 minutes to thicken the sauce slightly.

Garnish and Serve:
- Garnish with fresh sage leaves if desired. Serve the pork chops with the apple and sage sauce spooned over the top.

Enjoy:
- Serve the Apple and Sage Pork Chops hot, accompanied by your favorite side dishes.

This dish combines the savory flavors of sage-seasoned pork with the sweetness of caramelized apples, creating a delicious and comforting meal.

Apple and Cranberry Stuffed Acorn Squash

Ingredients:

- 2 acorn squash, halved and seeds removed
- 2 tablespoons olive oil
- Salt and black pepper, to taste
- 1 cup quinoa, rinsed and cooked according to package instructions
- 1 medium onion, finely chopped
- 2 cloves garlic, minced
- 1 medium apple, diced (use a sweet variety)
- 1/2 cup dried cranberries
- 1/2 cup chopped pecans or walnuts
- 1 teaspoon ground cinnamon
- 1/2 teaspoon ground nutmeg
- 1/4 cup fresh parsley, chopped
- 1/4 cup feta or goat cheese, crumbled (optional)
- Maple syrup, for drizzling (optional)

Instructions:

Preheat the Oven:
- Preheat your oven to 400°F (200°C).

Prepare Acorn Squash:
- Cut the acorn squash in half and remove the seeds. Place the squash halves on a baking sheet.

Drizzle with Olive Oil:
- Drizzle the inside of each acorn squash half with olive oil and season with salt and black pepper.

Roast Squash:
- Roast the acorn squash in the preheated oven for about 30-40 minutes or until the flesh is tender when pierced with a fork.

Prepare Quinoa:
- While the squash is roasting, cook the quinoa according to package instructions.

Saute Onion and Garlic:
- In a large skillet, heat a bit of olive oil over medium heat. Add chopped onion and sauté until softened. Add minced garlic and cook for an additional 1-2 minutes.

Combine Ingredients:
- Stir in the cooked quinoa, diced apple, dried cranberries, chopped nuts, ground cinnamon, ground nutmeg, and fresh parsley. Mix until well combined.

Stuff Acorn Squash:
- Once the acorn squash halves are done roasting, fill each half with the quinoa stuffing mixture.

Optional Cheese Topping:
- If desired, sprinkle crumbled feta or goat cheese on top of each stuffed squash half.

Return to Oven:
- Return the stuffed acorn squash to the oven and bake for an additional 10-15 minutes, or until the filling is heated through and the cheese is melted.

Drizzle with Maple Syrup (Optional):
- Before serving, drizzle with a bit of maple syrup for added sweetness if desired.

Serve:
- Serve the Apple and Cranberry Stuffed Acorn Squash warm, and enjoy!

This dish brings together the earthy flavor of acorn squash with the sweetness of apples and cranberries, creating a delightful and nutritious autumn-inspired meal

Apple Galette

Ingredients:

For the Dough:

- 1 1/4 cups all-purpose flour
- 1/2 teaspoon salt
- 1 tablespoon granulated sugar
- 1/2 cup unsalted butter, cold and cut into small cubes
- 3-4 tablespoons ice water

For the Filling:

- 3-4 medium-sized apples, thinly sliced (use a mix of sweet and tart varieties)
- 2 tablespoons granulated sugar
- 1 teaspoon ground cinnamon
- 1 tablespoon lemon juice
- Zest of one lemon

For Assembly:

- 1 tablespoon apricot preserves or apple jelly (for glazing)
- Powdered sugar, for dusting (optional)
- Vanilla ice cream or whipped cream, for serving (optional)

Instructions:

Prepare the Dough:

Mix Dry Ingredients:
- In a bowl, combine the all-purpose flour, salt, and granulated sugar.
Add Butter:
- Add the cold, cubed butter to the flour mixture. Use a pastry cutter or your fingers to incorporate the butter until the mixture resembles coarse crumbs.
Add Ice Water:

- Gradually add ice water, one tablespoon at a time, mixing until the dough just comes together. Be careful not to overmix.

Form a Disk:
- Gather the dough into a disk, wrap it in plastic wrap, and refrigerate for at least 30 minutes.

Prepare the Filling:

Prep Apples:
- Preheat the oven to 400°F (200°C). Thinly slice the apples and toss them with granulated sugar, ground cinnamon, lemon juice, and lemon zest.

Assemble the Galette:

Roll Out Dough:
- On a lightly floured surface, roll out the chilled dough into a circle, about 12 inches in diameter.

Transfer to Baking Sheet:
- Carefully transfer the rolled-out dough to a parchment paper-lined baking sheet.

Arrange Apple Slices:
- Arrange the sliced apples in the center of the dough, leaving a border around the edges.

Fold the Edges:
- Gently fold the edges of the dough over the apples, creating a rustic border.

Brush with Apricot Glaze:
- In a small saucepan, heat the apricot preserves or apple jelly until melted. Brush the melted preserves over the apples and the edges of the dough.

Bake:
- Bake in the preheated oven for 25-30 minutes or until the crust is golden brown and the apples are tender.

Cool and Dust with Powdered Sugar:
- Allow the galette to cool for a few minutes on the baking sheet. Optionally, dust with powdered sugar.

Serve:
- Serve the Apple Galette warm, and optionally, with a scoop of vanilla ice cream or a dollop of whipped cream.

This Apple Galette is a rustic and simple dessert that showcases the natural sweetness of apples. Enjoy the flaky crust and spiced apple filling!

Apple and Cinnamon Oatmeal

Ingredients:

- 1 cup old-fashioned rolled oats
- 2 cups water
- 1 cup milk (dairy or plant-based)
- 1 apple, peeled, cored, and diced
- 1-2 tablespoons maple syrup or honey (adjust to taste)
- 1/2 teaspoon ground cinnamon
- 1/4 teaspoon ground nutmeg (optional)
- Pinch of salt
- Toppings: Chopped nuts, raisins, sliced banana, or additional diced apples

Instructions:

Cook Oats:
- In a medium-sized saucepan, bring water to a boil. Stir in the rolled oats and reduce the heat to medium-low. Cook the oats, stirring occasionally, for about 5 minutes or until they reach your desired consistency.

Add Milk and Apple:
- Pour in the milk and add the diced apple to the cooking oats. Continue to cook for an additional 5-7 minutes, or until the apples are tender and the oatmeal is creamy.

Sweeten and Spice:
- Stir in maple syrup or honey, ground cinnamon, ground nutmeg (if using), and a pinch of salt. Adjust the sweetness and spice levels according to your preference.

Serve:
- Once the oatmeal reaches your desired consistency, remove it from the heat.

Toppings:
- Serve the Apple and Cinnamon Oatmeal hot, and top it with your favorite toppings such as chopped nuts, raisins, sliced banana, or additional diced apples.

Enjoy:
- Enjoy a warm and comforting bowl of Apple and Cinnamon Oatmeal as a delicious breakfast or snack.

Feel free to customize this oatmeal by adding your favorite toppings or adjusting the sweetness and spice levels. It's a wholesome and nutritious way to start your day!

Apple and Gouda Grilled Cheese

Ingredients:

- 8 slices of bread (your choice of bread)
- 8 ounces Gouda cheese, thinly sliced
- 1-2 apples, thinly sliced (use a sweet variety like Honeycrisp or Fuji)
- Butter, softened
- Dijon mustard (optional)
- Honey (optional)

Instructions:

Preheat Griddle or Skillet:
- Preheat a griddle or non-stick skillet over medium heat.

Assemble the Sandwiches:
- Lay out 8 slices of bread. On 4 slices, evenly distribute the Gouda cheese slices. Top the cheese with a layer of thinly sliced apples.

Optional Condiments:
- If desired, spread a thin layer of Dijon mustard on the remaining 4 slices of bread. Drizzle honey over the apples for added sweetness if you like.

Create Sandwiches:
- Place the Dijon mustard or honey-drizzled slices on top of the apple and cheese slices to create sandwiches.

Butter the Bread:
- Lightly spread softened butter on the outer sides of each sandwich.

Grill the Sandwiches:
- Place the sandwiches on the preheated griddle or skillet. Cook for 3-4 minutes on each side, or until the bread is golden brown, and the cheese is melted.

Pressing the Sandwich:
- If you have a sandwich press or a heavy skillet, you can place it on top of the sandwiches while they cook to press them down and help the cheese melt.

Serve:
- Once the sandwiches are grilled to perfection, remove them from the griddle or skillet. Allow them to cool for a minute before slicing.

Enjoy:

- Serve the Apple and Gouda Grilled Cheese sandwiches warm and enjoy the gooey cheese, sweet apples, and savory flavors.

This grilled cheese combines the rich and creamy flavor of Gouda with the sweetness of apples for a delightful twist on a classic sandwich. Feel free to experiment with different bread varieties to suit your taste!

Apple and Almond Smoothie

Ingredients:

- 1 medium-sized apple, cored and chopped
- 1/4 cup almonds, preferably soaked and blanched
- 1/2 cup Greek yogurt or plant-based yogurt
- 1/2 cup almond milk or any milk of your choice
- 1 tablespoon honey or maple syrup (adjust to taste)
- 1/2 teaspoon ground cinnamon
- Ice cubes (optional)
- Almond slices for garnish (optional)

Instructions:

Prepare Ingredients:
- If you haven't already, soak and blanch the almonds. To blanch, pour hot water over the almonds and let them sit for a few minutes. Then, remove the skins by gently squeezing each almond.

Blend:
- In a blender, combine the chopped apple, soaked and blanched almonds, Greek yogurt, almond milk, honey or maple syrup, and ground cinnamon.

Blend Until Smooth:
- Blend the ingredients until smooth and creamy. If the smoothie is too thick, you can add more almond milk to reach your desired consistency.

Add Ice Cubes (Optional):
- If you prefer a colder smoothie, you can add a handful of ice cubes and blend again until the ice is crushed and the smoothie is well-chilled.

Taste and Adjust:
- Taste the smoothie and adjust the sweetness by adding more honey or maple syrup if needed.

Serve:
- Pour the Apple and Almond Smoothie into glasses.

Garnish (Optional):
- Optionally, garnish with almond slices on top for added texture.

Enjoy:
- Enjoy this nutritious and flavorful Apple and Almond Smoothie as a refreshing breakfast or snack!

This smoothie combines the natural sweetness of apples with the nutty richness of almonds, creating a satisfying and wholesome drink. Feel free to customize it by adding your favorite smoothie ingredients or adjusting the sweetness to suit your taste.

Apple and Sausage Stuffed Mushrooms

Ingredients:

- 20 large white mushrooms, cleaned and stems removed
- 1 tablespoon olive oil
- 1/2 pound (about 225g) ground sausage (pork or turkey)
- 1 small onion, finely chopped
- 1 medium apple, finely diced (use a sweet variety)
- 1/3 cup breadcrumbs
- 1/4 cup grated Parmesan cheese
- 2 tablespoons fresh parsley, chopped
- Salt and pepper, to taste
- 2 tablespoons unsalted butter, melted

Instructions:

Preheat the Oven:
- Preheat your oven to 375°F (190°C).

Prepare Mushrooms:
- Clean the mushrooms and remove the stems. Place the mushroom caps on a baking sheet lined with parchment paper.

Saute Sausage and Vegetables:
- In a skillet, heat olive oil over medium heat. Add the ground sausage and cook until browned. Add chopped onion and cook until softened. Stir in diced apple and cook for an additional 2-3 minutes until the apple is slightly tender.

Make the Filling:
- Remove the skillet from heat. In a bowl, combine the cooked sausage mixture with breadcrumbs, grated Parmesan cheese, chopped parsley, salt, and pepper. Mix well.

Stuff the Mushrooms:
- Using a spoon, stuff each mushroom cap with the sausage and apple mixture, pressing down gently to pack the filling.

Brush with Butter:
- Brush the tops of the stuffed mushrooms with melted butter.

Bake:

- Bake in the preheated oven for about 20-25 minutes or until the mushrooms are tender and the filling is golden brown.

Serve:
- Remove from the oven and let them cool slightly. Serve the Apple and Sausage Stuffed Mushrooms warm.

Enjoy:
- Enjoy these savory and flavorful stuffed mushrooms as a delightful appetizer or party snack!

These stuffed mushrooms offer a perfect combination of savory sausage, sweet apple, and the earthy flavor of mushrooms. They make a great addition to any gathering or as an appetizer for a cozy dinner at home.

Apple and Cinnamon Pull-Apart Bread

Ingredients:

For the Dough:

- 2 1/4 teaspoons (1 packet) active dry yeast
- 1 cup warm milk (about 110°F/43°C)
- 1/4 cup granulated sugar
- 1/3 cup unsalted butter, melted
- 1 teaspoon vanilla extract
- 3 1/2 cups all-purpose flour
- 1/2 teaspoon salt

For the Filling:

- 1/2 cup unsalted butter, softened
- 1/2 cup brown sugar, packed
- 2 teaspoons ground cinnamon
- 2 medium-sized apples, peeled, cored, and finely diced

For the Glaze:

- 1 cup powdered sugar
- 2 tablespoons milk
- 1/2 teaspoon vanilla extract

Instructions:

Prepare the Dough:

Activate Yeast:
- In a bowl, combine warm milk and sugar. Sprinkle the active dry yeast over the milk mixture, stir gently, and let it sit for about 5-10 minutes until it becomes frothy.

Mix Dough Ingredients:
- In a large mixing bowl, combine the yeast mixture, melted butter, vanilla extract, flour, and salt. Mix until a dough forms.

Knead and Rise:

- Turn the dough out onto a floured surface and knead for about 5-7 minutes until it becomes smooth and elastic. Place the dough in a greased bowl, cover with a clean kitchen towel, and let it rise in a warm place for about 1-2 hours, or until doubled in size.

Prepare the Filling:

Mix Filling Ingredients:
- In a small bowl, mix together the softened butter, brown sugar, and ground cinnamon until well combined.

Prepare Apples:
- Peel, core, and finely dice the apples.

Assemble the Pull-Apart Bread:

Roll Out Dough:
- Roll out the risen dough on a floured surface into a rectangle, approximately 12x18 inches.

Spread Filling:
- Spread the cinnamon-brown sugar filling evenly over the entire surface of the rolled-out dough. Sprinkle the diced apples over the filling.

Cut into Strips:
- Using a pizza cutter or a sharp knife, cut the dough into strips (about 6-8 strips).

Stack Strips:
- Stack the strips on top of each other to create a layered stack.

Cut into Squares:
- Cut the stacked dough into squares, creating small stacks of layered squares.

Place in Pan:
- Place the stacks of dough squares in a greased loaf pan.

Let it Rise:
- Cover the pan with a kitchen towel and let the dough rise for an additional 30 minutes.

Bake:
- Preheat the oven to 350°F (180°C). Bake the pull-apart bread for 30-35 minutes, or until golden brown.

Prepare the Glaze:

Mix Glaze Ingredients:
- In a bowl, whisk together powdered sugar, milk, and vanilla extract until smooth.

Drizzle Glaze:
- Once the pull-apart bread has cooled slightly, drizzle the glaze over the top.

Serve:
- Serve the Apple and Cinnamon Pull-Apart Bread warm. Pull apart the layers and enjoy!

This Apple and Cinnamon Pull-Apart Bread is a delightful treat with layers of sweetness and warmth. It's perfect for sharing with family and friends.

Apple and Caramelized Onion Pizza

Ingredients:

For the Pizza Dough:

- 1 pound (about 4 cups) pizza dough, homemade or store-bought

For the Toppings:

- 1 large red onion, thinly sliced
- 2 tablespoons olive oil
- 1 tablespoon balsamic vinegar
- 1 tablespoon brown sugar
- 2 apples, thinly sliced (use a sweet variety like Honeycrisp or Fuji)
- 1 1/2 cups shredded mozzarella cheese
- 1/2 cup crumbled goat cheese
- Fresh thyme leaves for garnish
- Salt and black pepper to taste

For the Caramelized Walnuts (Optional):

- 1/2 cup walnuts, roughly chopped
- 2 tablespoons butter
- 2 tablespoons brown sugar

Instructions:

Prepare the Pizza Dough:

Preheat Oven:
- Preheat your oven according to the pizza dough instructions or around 475°F (245°C).

Caramelize Onions:
- In a skillet over medium heat, heat 2 tablespoons of olive oil. Add the thinly sliced red onions and cook until they start to soften. Stir in balsamic vinegar and brown sugar. Continue cooking, stirring occasionally, until the

onions are caramelized and golden brown. Remove from heat and set aside.

Prepare Caramelized Walnuts (Optional):

- In a small pan over medium heat, melt 2 tablespoons of butter. Add chopped walnuts and brown sugar. Stir continuously until the walnuts are caramelized. Remove from heat and set aside.

Roll Out Pizza Dough:

- Roll out the pizza dough on a floured surface to your desired thickness.

Assemble the Pizza:

- Transfer the rolled-out pizza dough to a pizza stone or baking sheet. Spread the caramelized onions evenly over the dough. Arrange the sliced apples on top. Sprinkle the shredded mozzarella cheese and crumbled goat cheese over the apples.

Optional Caramelized Walnuts:

- If using caramelized walnuts, sprinkle them over the pizza.

Season and Bake:

- Season the pizza with salt and black pepper. Bake in the preheated oven according to the pizza dough instructions or until the crust is golden brown and the cheese is melted and bubbly.

Garnish:

- Remove the pizza from the oven and garnish with fresh thyme leaves.

Serve:

- Slice the Apple and Caramelized Onion Pizza and serve hot. Enjoy!

This pizza combines the sweetness of caramelized onions and apples with the tanginess of goat cheese, creating a delicious and unique flavor profile. The optional caramelized walnuts add a delightful crunch. Perfect for a cozy night in or a special dinner!

Apple and Cranberry Baked Brie

Ingredients:

- 1 wheel of Brie cheese (about 8 ounces)
- 1 sheet of puff pastry, thawed
- 1/2 cup cranberry sauce (homemade or store-bought)
- 1 medium-sized apple, thinly sliced
- 1 tablespoon honey
- 1 tablespoon chopped pecans or walnuts (optional)
- 1 egg (beaten, for egg wash)
- Crackers or bread, for serving

Instructions:

Preheat the Oven:
- Preheat your oven to 375°F (190°C).

Prepare the Brie:
- If the Brie has a rind on it, you can choose to leave it on or remove the top layer. If you're leaving it on, score the top of the Brie with a sharp knife in a criss-cross pattern.

Roll Out Puff Pastry:
- On a lightly floured surface, roll out the puff pastry sheet to a size large enough to wrap around the Brie.

Wrap Brie with Puff Pastry:
- Place the Brie in the center of the rolled-out puff pastry. Spread a layer of cranberry sauce over the top of the Brie. Arrange thinly sliced apples over the cranberry sauce. Drizzle honey on top and sprinkle with chopped nuts if using.

Encase Brie in Pastry:
- Gently fold the puff pastry over the Brie, sealing the edges. Trim any excess pastry if needed.

Brush with Egg Wash:
- Brush the entire surface of the puff pastry with the beaten egg. This will give it a golden brown color when baked.

Bake:

- Place the wrapped Brie on a baking sheet or in a Brie baker. Bake in the preheated oven for 20-25 minutes, or until the pastry is golden brown and the Brie is soft and gooey.

Serve:
- Remove from the oven and let it cool for a few minutes. Serve the Apple and Cranberry Baked Brie with crackers or slices of bread.

Enjoy:
- Enjoy this delicious appetizer with a perfect blend of creamy Brie, sweet cranberry, and crisp apple flavors!

This Apple and Cranberry Baked Brie is a fantastic appetizer for holiday gatherings or any special occasion. The combination of melted cheese, fruity sweetness, and the flaky pastry creates a delightful treat for your taste buds.

Apple and Cinnamon Scones

Ingredients:

- 2 cups all-purpose flour
- 1/4 cup granulated sugar
- 1 tablespoon baking powder
- 1/2 teaspoon salt
- 1 teaspoon ground cinnamon
- 1/2 cup unsalted butter, cold and cut into small pieces
- 1 large apple, peeled, cored, and diced
- 1/2 cup buttermilk
- 1 teaspoon vanilla extract
- 1 large egg (for egg wash)
- Cinnamon sugar (for sprinkling)

Instructions:

Preheat the Oven:
- Preheat your oven to 400°F (200°C). Line a baking sheet with parchment paper.

Mix Dry Ingredients:
- In a large bowl, whisk together the flour, sugar, baking powder, salt, and ground cinnamon.

Cut in Butter:
- Add the cold, diced butter to the dry ingredients. Using a pastry cutter or your fingers, cut the butter into the flour mixture until it resembles coarse crumbs.

Add Apple:
- Gently fold in the diced apple into the flour mixture.

Combine Wet Ingredients:
- In a separate bowl, whisk together the buttermilk and vanilla extract.

Form Dough:
- Make a well in the center of the dry ingredients and pour in the wet ingredients. Stir until just combined. Be careful not to overmix.

Shape Dough:
- Turn the dough out onto a floured surface and gently knead it a few times. Pat the dough into a circle about 1 inch thick.

Cut Scones:

- Using a floured round cutter or a sharp knife, cut out scones from the dough. Place the scones on the prepared baking sheet.

Egg Wash:

- In a small bowl, beat the egg. Brush the tops of the scones with the beaten egg.

Sprinkle Cinnamon Sugar:

- Sprinkle the tops of the scones with cinnamon sugar for a sweet finish.

Bake:

- Bake in the preheated oven for 12-15 minutes or until the scones are golden brown.

Cool:

- Allow the scones to cool on a wire rack for a few minutes before serving.

Enjoy:

- Serve these delicious Apple and Cinnamon Scones warm with clotted cream, butter, or your favorite jam.

These scones are perfect for a cozy breakfast or afternoon tea. The combination of sweet apples and warm cinnamon creates a delightful treat that's sure to be enjoyed by everyone!

Apple and Pecan Stuffed Pork Tenderloin

Ingredients:

For the Pork:

- 2 pork tenderloins (about 1 to 1.5 pounds each)
- Salt and black pepper, to taste
- 1 tablespoon olive oil

For the Stuffing:

- 2 cups apples, peeled and finely chopped (such as Granny Smith or Honeycrisp)
- 1/2 cup pecans, chopped
- 1/4 cup dried cranberries
- 2 tablespoons brown sugar
- 1 teaspoon ground cinnamon
- 1/4 teaspoon ground nutmeg
- Salt, to taste

For the Glaze:

- 1/4 cup apple cider or apple juice
- 2 tablespoons maple syrup
- 1 tablespoon Dijon mustard

Instructions:

Preheat the Oven:
- Preheat your oven to 375°F (190°C).

Prepare the Pork Tenderloins:
- Trim any excess fat from the pork tenderloins. Season them with salt and black pepper.

Butterfly the Pork:
- Butterfly the pork tenderloins by making a lengthwise cut down the center, being careful not to cut all the way through. Open the pork like a book.

Prepare the Stuffing:
- In a bowl, combine chopped apples, pecans, dried cranberries, brown sugar, ground cinnamon, ground nutmeg, and a pinch of salt. Mix well to combine.

Stuff the Pork:
- Spread the stuffing evenly over the opened pork tenderloins. Fold the pork back together, enclosing the stuffing. Tie the tenderloins with kitchen twine to secure the stuffing.

Sear the Pork:
- In an oven-safe skillet, heat olive oil over medium-high heat. Sear the stuffed pork tenderloins on all sides until browned.

Prepare the Glaze:
- In a small bowl, whisk together apple cider (or apple juice), maple syrup, and Dijon mustard.

Brush with Glaze:
- Brush the glaze over the seared pork tenderloins.

Roast in the Oven:
- Transfer the skillet to the preheated oven and roast for about 20-25 minutes or until the internal temperature of the pork reaches 145°F (63°C).

Rest and Slice:
- Remove the pork from the oven and let it rest for a few minutes before slicing. Remove the kitchen twine before slicing into rounds.

Serve:
- Serve the Apple and Pecan Stuffed Pork Tenderloin slices with any remaining glaze drizzled over the top.

Enjoy:
- Enjoy this flavorful and festive stuffed pork dish with your favorite side dishes!

This Apple and Pecan Stuffed Pork Tenderloin is a perfect combination of sweet and savory flavors, making it an excellent choice for a special dinner or holiday meal.

Apple and Goat Cheese Crostini

Ingredients:

- Baguette or French bread, sliced into 1/2-inch thick rounds
- Olive oil, for brushing
- 4 ounces (about 1/2 cup) goat cheese, softened
- 2 medium-sized apples, thinly sliced (such as Honeycrisp or Granny Smith)
- Honey, for drizzling
- Fresh thyme leaves, for garnish
- Crushed black pepper, for garnish

Instructions:

Preheat the Oven:
- Preheat your oven to 375°F (190°C).

Prepare the Crostini:
- Place the baguette slices on a baking sheet. Brush each slice lightly with olive oil. Bake in the preheated oven for about 8-10 minutes or until the edges are golden brown.

Spread Goat Cheese:
- Once the crostini slices are toasted, spread a generous amount of goat cheese on each slice while they are still warm.

Add Apple Slices:
- Place a few slices of thinly sliced apples on top of the goat cheese.

Drizzle with Honey:
- Drizzle honey over the apple slices. The sweetness of honey complements the tanginess of the goat cheese and the crispness of the apples.

Garnish:
- Sprinkle fresh thyme leaves over the crostini for a burst of flavor. Add a touch of crushed black pepper for some extra depth.

Serve:
- Arrange the Apple and Goat Cheese Crostini on a serving platter and serve immediately.

Enjoy:
- Enjoy these delightful bites with a perfect balance of creamy goat cheese, sweet apples, and a drizzle of honey. They make an excellent appetizer for gatherings or a tasty snack.

This Apple and Goat Cheese Crostini recipe is not only delicious but also visually appealing, making it a great choice for entertaining or as an elegant appetizer before a meal.

Apple and Cranberry Chutney

Ingredients:

- 2 cups fresh cranberries
- 2 medium-sized apples, peeled, cored, and chopped
- 1 cup granulated sugar
- 1/2 cup brown sugar, packed
- 1/2 cup apple cider vinegar
- 1/2 cup water
- 1 teaspoon ground cinnamon
- 1/2 teaspoon ground ginger
- 1/4 teaspoon ground cloves
- 1/4 teaspoon salt
- Zest and juice of 1 orange
- 1/2 cup chopped walnuts or pecans (optional)

Instructions:

Prepare Ingredients:
- Rinse the cranberries and chop the apples.

Cook Cranberries and Apples:
- In a medium-sized saucepan, combine cranberries, chopped apples, granulated sugar, brown sugar, apple cider vinegar, water, ground cinnamon, ground ginger, ground cloves, and salt.

Bring to a Boil:
- Bring the mixture to a boil over medium-high heat, stirring occasionally.

Simmer:
- Reduce the heat to low and let the chutney simmer for about 15-20 minutes or until the cranberries burst and the apples are tender.

Add Orange Zest and Juice:
- Stir in the orange zest and juice. Continue to simmer for an additional 5-10 minutes until the chutney thickens.

Optional Nuts:
- If using nuts, stir in the chopped walnuts or pecans during the last 5 minutes of cooking.

Cool and Serve:
- Remove the chutney from heat and let it cool to room temperature. The chutney will thicken as it cools.

Store:
- Transfer the Apple and Cranberry Chutney to a jar or airtight container. Refrigerate until ready to serve.

Serve:
- Serve the chutney as a condiment with roasted meats, on a cheese platter, or as a delightful accompaniment to holiday dishes.

Enjoy:
- Enjoy the sweet and tangy flavors of this Apple and Cranberry Chutney, adding a burst of festive taste to your meals!

This chutney is a versatile condiment that can elevate both savory and sweet dishes. It's particularly wonderful during the holiday season and can be made in advance for convenience.

Apple and Cinnamon Granola

Ingredients:

- 3 cups old-fashioned rolled oats
- 1 cup chopped nuts (such as almonds, walnuts, or pecans)
- 1/2 cup unsweetened shredded coconut
- 1/2 cup dried cranberries or raisins
- 1/2 cup dried apple slices, chopped
- 1/3 cup coconut oil, melted
- 1/4 cup pure maple syrup or honey
- 1 teaspoon ground cinnamon
- 1/2 teaspoon vanilla extract
- 1/4 teaspoon salt

Instructions:

Preheat the Oven:
- Preheat your oven to 325°F (163°C). Line a baking sheet with parchment paper.

Mix Dry Ingredients:
- In a large bowl, combine the rolled oats, chopped nuts, shredded coconut, dried cranberries (or raisins), and dried apple slices.

Prepare Wet Ingredients:
- In a separate bowl, whisk together melted coconut oil, maple syrup (or honey), ground cinnamon, vanilla extract, and salt.

Combine Wet and Dry Ingredients:
- Pour the wet ingredients over the dry ingredients and stir until everything is well coated.

Spread on Baking Sheet:
- Spread the granola mixture evenly onto the prepared baking sheet.

Bake:
- Bake in the preheated oven for about 25-30 minutes, stirring every 10 minutes to ensure even browning.

Cool Completely:
- Once the granola is golden brown and fragrant, remove it from the oven and allow it to cool completely on the baking sheet. It will continue to crisp up as it cools.

Store:

- Transfer the cooled Apple and Cinnamon Granola to an airtight container for storage.

Serve:

- Serve the granola with yogurt, milk, or as a topping for fruit salads. Enjoy it as a nutritious breakfast or snack!

Optional: Additions

- Feel free to customize your granola by adding other ingredients such as chia seeds, flaxseeds, or additional dried fruits.

This Apple and Cinnamon Granola is a wholesome and flavorful way to start your day. It's also great for snacking and can be a lovely homemade gift when packaged in a decorative jar.

Apple and Cider Glazed Chicken

Ingredients:

- 4 boneless, skinless chicken breasts
- Salt and black pepper, to taste
- 2 tablespoons olive oil
- 1 cup apple cider
- 1/4 cup apple cider vinegar
- 1/4 cup maple syrup
- 2 tablespoons Dijon mustard
- 2 cloves garlic, minced
- 1 teaspoon fresh thyme leaves (or 1/2 teaspoon dried thyme)
- 1/2 teaspoon ground cinnamon
- 1/4 teaspoon ground nutmeg
- Chopped fresh parsley, for garnish (optional)

Instructions:

Season the Chicken:
- Season the chicken breasts with salt and black pepper on both sides.

Sear the Chicken:
- In a large skillet, heat olive oil over medium-high heat. Add the chicken breasts and sear for 3-4 minutes on each side or until golden brown. Remove the chicken from the skillet and set aside.

Prepare the Glaze:
- In the same skillet, add apple cider, apple cider vinegar, maple syrup, Dijon mustard, minced garlic, thyme, cinnamon, and nutmeg. Stir to combine.

Simmer:
- Bring the mixture to a simmer and let it cook for about 5-7 minutes or until the sauce thickens slightly.

Return Chicken to the Skillet:
- Return the seared chicken breasts to the skillet, spooning the glaze over them.

Cook Through:
- Continue to cook the chicken in the glaze for an additional 10-15 minutes or until the internal temperature reaches 165°F (74°C) and the chicken is cooked through. Baste the chicken with the glaze occasionally.

Garnish and Serve:
- Once the chicken is cooked, remove it from the skillet. Garnish with chopped fresh parsley if desired.

Reduce Glaze (Optional):
- If the glaze needs further thickening, continue to simmer it for a few more minutes until it reaches your desired consistency.

Serve:
- Serve the Apple and Cider Glazed Chicken over rice, quinoa, or with your favorite side dishes. Drizzle extra glaze over the chicken before serving.

Enjoy:
- Enjoy this flavorful and autumn-inspired dish with the sweet and tangy glaze!

This Apple and Cider Glazed Chicken is a perfect combination of savory and sweet flavors, making it a delightful and comforting meal for any occasion.

Apple and Thyme Roasted Turkey

Ingredients:

- 1 whole turkey (12-15 pounds), thawed if frozen
- Salt and black pepper, to taste
- 1 cup unsalted butter, softened
- 2 apples, sliced (such as Granny Smith or Honeycrisp)
- 1 onion, quartered
- 4-5 sprigs of fresh thyme
- 4 cloves garlic, minced
- 1 cup apple cider or apple juice
- 1 cup chicken or turkey broth
- 1/4 cup maple syrup
- 2 tablespoons Dijon mustard
- 1 teaspoon ground cinnamon
- 1/2 teaspoon ground nutmeg
- 1/2 teaspoon dried sage
- 1/2 teaspoon dried rosemary

Instructions:

Preheat the Oven:
- Preheat your oven to 325°F (163°C).

Prepare the Turkey:
- Remove the turkey from its packaging. Pat it dry with paper towels. Season the cavity and the skin of the turkey generously with salt and black pepper.

Make Herb Butter:
- In a small bowl, mix together softened butter, minced garlic, ground cinnamon, ground nutmeg, dried sage, and dried rosemary. Set aside.

Herb Butter Under the Skin:
- Gently loosen the skin from the turkey breast. Rub half of the herb butter mixture under the skin, directly onto the meat.

Herb Butter Over the Skin:
- Rub the remaining herb butter over the outside of the turkey.

Stuff the Cavity:
- Place sliced apples, quartered onion, and fresh thyme sprigs into the turkey cavity.

Tie Legs:

- If the turkey legs are not pre-tied, use kitchen twine to tie them together.

Prepare the Glaze:

- In a saucepan, combine apple cider, chicken or turkey broth, maple syrup, and Dijon mustard. Bring the mixture to a simmer over medium heat. Let it simmer for about 5 minutes.

Roast the Turkey:

- Place the turkey on a rack in a roasting pan. Pour half of the glaze over the turkey.

Basting:

- Roast the turkey in the preheated oven, basting every 30 minutes with the remaining glaze, until the internal temperature reaches 165°F (74°C) in the thickest part of the thigh.

Cover if Needed:

- If the skin is browning too quickly, cover the turkey with foil.

Rest and Carve:

- Once the turkey is cooked, let it rest for at least 20-30 minutes before carving.

Serve:

- Serve the Apple and Thyme Roasted Turkey slices with your favorite sides and enjoy!

This Apple and Thyme Roasted Turkey is not only flavorful but also beautifully aromatic. The combination of apples, thyme, and a hint of maple syrup creates a deliciously festive turkey perfect for holidays or special occasions.

Apple and Cinnamon Energy Balls

Ingredients:

- 1 cup rolled oats
- 1/2 cup unsweetened applesauce
- 1/2 cup almond butter (or any nut/seed butter of your choice)
- 1/4 cup honey or maple syrup
- 1 teaspoon ground cinnamon
- 1/2 teaspoon vanilla extract
- Pinch of salt
- 1/2 cup shredded coconut (optional, for coating)

Instructions:

Combine Dry Ingredients:
- In a mixing bowl, combine rolled oats, ground cinnamon, and a pinch of salt.

Add Wet Ingredients:
- Add applesauce, almond butter, honey (or maple syrup), and vanilla extract to the dry ingredients.

Mix Well:
- Mix the ingredients thoroughly until well combined. The mixture should be sticky and hold together.

Chill in the Refrigerator:
- Place the mixture in the refrigerator for about 30 minutes. Chilling helps the mixture firm up, making it easier to shape into balls.

Shape into Balls:
- Once chilled, take small portions of the mixture and roll them into bite-sized balls using your hands. If the mixture is too sticky, you can lightly wet your hands.

Optional Coconut Coating:
- If desired, roll the energy balls in shredded coconut to coat them.

Store:
- Place the Apple and Cinnamon Energy Balls on a parchment-lined tray and refrigerate for at least another 30 minutes to set.

Enjoy:

- Once set, your energy balls are ready to enjoy! Store them in an airtight container in the refrigerator for longer shelf life.

These Apple and Cinnamon Energy Balls make for a healthy and satisfying snack. They are packed with wholesome ingredients and the delightful flavors of apple and cinnamon. They are convenient to grab when you need a quick energy boost during the day.

Apple and Rosemary Roasted Vegetables

Ingredients:

- 4 cups mixed vegetables, cut into bite-sized pieces (such as carrots, sweet potatoes, Brussels sprouts, and red onions)
- 2 medium-sized apples, cored and sliced
- 3 tablespoons olive oil
- 2 tablespoons balsamic vinegar
- 1 tablespoon honey
- 2 teaspoons fresh rosemary, chopped
- Salt and black pepper, to taste

Instructions:

Preheat the Oven:
- Preheat your oven to 400°F (200°C).

Prepare Vegetables:
- Wash and cut the vegetables into bite-sized pieces. If using Brussels sprouts, trim the ends and cut them in half.

Mix Olive Oil and Balsamic Vinegar:
- In a small bowl, whisk together olive oil, balsamic vinegar, honey, chopped rosemary, salt, and black pepper.

Coat Vegetables:
- Place the mixed vegetables and apple slices in a large bowl. Pour the olive oil and balsamic mixture over the vegetables and toss until well coated.

Spread on Baking Sheet:
- Spread the coated vegetables and apples in a single layer on a baking sheet. Ensure they are evenly spaced for even roasting.

Roast in the Oven:
- Roast in the preheated oven for 25-30 minutes or until the vegetables are tender and caramelized, stirring halfway through the roasting time.

Serve:
- Once roasted to your liking, remove the vegetables from the oven.

Garnish (Optional):
- Garnish with additional fresh rosemary if desired.

Serve Warm:
- Serve the Apple and Rosemary Roasted Vegetables warm as a delicious side dish.

Enjoy:

- Enjoy this flavorful and aromatic dish that combines the sweetness of apples with the earthiness of rosemary, creating a delightful roasted vegetable medley.

This dish not only adds a burst of flavors to your meal but also makes a beautiful and colorful addition to your table. It's perfect for autumn or any time you want a comforting and nutritious side dish.

Apple and Cranberry Quinoa Salad

Ingredients:

- 1 cup quinoa, rinsed
- 2 cups water or vegetable broth
- 1 large apple, diced (such as Honeycrisp or Granny Smith)
- 1/2 cup dried cranberries
- 1/2 cup chopped pecans or walnuts
- 1/3 cup crumbled feta cheese (optional)
- 1/4 cup fresh parsley, chopped
- 2 tablespoons extra-virgin olive oil
- 2 tablespoons balsamic vinegar
- 1 tablespoon maple syrup or honey
- Salt and black pepper, to taste

Instructions:

Cook Quinoa:
- In a medium saucepan, combine quinoa and water or vegetable broth. Bring to a boil, then reduce the heat to low, cover, and simmer for 15-20 minutes or until the quinoa is cooked and the liquid is absorbed. Fluff the quinoa with a fork and let it cool.

Prepare Dressing:
- In a small bowl, whisk together olive oil, balsamic vinegar, maple syrup (or honey), salt, and black pepper to create the dressing.

Assemble Salad:
- In a large bowl, combine the cooked quinoa, diced apple, dried cranberries, chopped nuts, and crumbled feta cheese (if using).

Add Dressing:
- Pour the dressing over the salad and toss gently to combine, ensuring that all ingredients are well coated.

Garnish:
- Garnish the salad with chopped fresh parsley.

Chill (Optional):
- Refrigerate the salad for at least 30 minutes to allow the flavors to meld. This step is optional but can enhance the taste.

Serve:

- Serve the Apple and Cranberry Quinoa Salad as a refreshing side dish or a light meal.

Enjoy:

- Enjoy the delightful combination of sweet apples, tart cranberries, and nutty quinoa in this nutritious and flavorful salad.

This salad is not only delicious but also packed with protein and nutrients, making it a perfect option for a healthy lunch or a side dish for dinner. It's a great way to enjoy the vibrant flavors of fall.

Apple and Cinnamon French Toast

Ingredients:

For the French Toast:

- 4 large eggs
- 1 cup milk
- 1 teaspoon ground cinnamon
- 1/2 teaspoon vanilla extract
- 8 slices of your favorite bread (such as brioche or French bread)
- Butter for cooking

For the Apple Topping:

- 2 medium-sized apples, peeled, cored, and thinly sliced
- 2 tablespoons unsalted butter
- 2 tablespoons brown sugar
- 1/2 teaspoon ground cinnamon
- Pinch of salt

Optional Toppings:

- Maple syrup
- Powdered sugar
- Chopped nuts (such as pecans or walnuts)

Instructions:

Prepare the Egg Mixture:
- In a shallow bowl, whisk together eggs, milk, ground cinnamon, and vanilla extract.

Dip the Bread:
- Dip each slice of bread into the egg mixture, ensuring it is well-coated on both sides.

Cook the French Toast:
- In a skillet or griddle, melt a bit of butter over medium heat. Cook the dipped bread slices for 2-3 minutes on each side or until golden brown.

Keep Warm:

- Keep the cooked French toast warm in a preheated oven while you prepare the apple topping.

Prepare the Apple Topping:
- In a separate pan, melt butter over medium heat. Add sliced apples, brown sugar, ground cinnamon, and a pinch of salt. Cook for 5-7 minutes or until the apples are tender and caramelized.

Assemble:
- Place a generous spoonful of the cooked apple topping over each slice of French toast.

Optional Toppings:
- Drizzle with maple syrup, sprinkle with chopped nuts, and dust with powdered sugar if desired.

Serve:
- Serve the Apple and Cinnamon French Toast warm and enjoy!

This Apple and Cinnamon French Toast is a perfect combination of soft, eggy bread with the sweet and spiced flavor of caramelized apples. It's a delightful breakfast or brunch option, especially during the fall season.

Apple and Walnut Chicken Salad

Ingredients:

For the Chicken:

- 2 boneless, skinless chicken breasts
- Salt and black pepper, to taste
- 1 tablespoon olive oil
- 1 teaspoon dried thyme (or 1 tablespoon fresh thyme)

For the Salad:

- 4 cups mixed salad greens (lettuce, spinach, arugula, etc.)
- 2 apples, cored and sliced (such as Honeycrisp or Granny Smith)
- 1 cup red seedless grapes, halved
- 1/2 cup chopped walnuts, toasted
- 1/2 cup crumbled feta cheese (optional)

For the Dressing:

- 3 tablespoons olive oil
- 2 tablespoons apple cider vinegar
- 1 tablespoon Dijon mustard
- 1 tablespoon honey
- Salt and black pepper, to taste

Instructions:

Prepare the Chicken:
- Season the chicken breasts with salt, black pepper, and dried thyme on both sides. In a skillet, heat olive oil over medium-high heat. Cook the chicken for 5-7 minutes per side or until cooked through. Let it rest for a few minutes before slicing.

Make the Dressing:
- In a small bowl, whisk together olive oil, apple cider vinegar, Dijon mustard, honey, salt, and black pepper to create the dressing.

Toast the Walnuts:
- In a dry skillet, toast the chopped walnuts over medium heat for 3-4 minutes or until fragrant. Be careful not to burn them.

Assemble the Salad:
- In a large bowl, combine the mixed salad greens, sliced apples, halved grapes, and toasted walnuts.

Slice the Chicken:
- Slice the cooked chicken breasts into thin strips.

Add Chicken and Feta (Optional):
- Add the sliced chicken to the salad. If desired, sprinkle crumbled feta cheese over the top.

Drizzle with Dressing:
- Drizzle the salad with the prepared dressing and toss gently to combine, ensuring everything is well coated.

Serve:
- Serve the Apple and Walnut Chicken Salad immediately and enjoy!

This salad offers a delightful combination of tender chicken, crisp apples, sweet grapes, and crunchy walnuts, all tied together with a flavorful dressing. It's a perfect light and satisfying meal, especially during the warmer seasons.

Apple and Caramel Bread Pudding

Ingredients:

- 6 cups cubed bread (day-old bread works well)
- 2 large apples, peeled, cored, and diced (such as Granny Smith or Honeycrisp)
- 1/2 cup raisins or dried cranberries (optional)
- 4 large eggs
- 2 cups whole milk
- 1 cup heavy cream
- 1 cup granulated sugar
- 1 teaspoon vanilla extract
- 1/2 teaspoon ground cinnamon
- 1/4 teaspoon ground nutmeg
- 1/2 cup caramel sauce (store-bought or homemade)
- Powdered sugar for dusting (optional)

Instructions:

Preheat the Oven:
- Preheat your oven to 350°F (175°C). Grease a 9x13-inch baking dish.

Prepare Bread and Apples:
- In a large bowl, combine the cubed bread, diced apples, and raisins or dried cranberries if using. Spread this mixture evenly in the prepared baking dish.

Make Custard Mixture:
- In another bowl, whisk together eggs, whole milk, heavy cream, granulated sugar, vanilla extract, ground cinnamon, and ground nutmeg until well combined.

Pour Custard Over Bread Mixture:
- Pour the custard mixture evenly over the bread and apples in the baking dish. Press down slightly to ensure the bread absorbs the liquid.

Let it Soak:
- Allow the bread mixture to soak in the custard for about 15-20 minutes, occasionally pressing down gently.

Drizzle with Caramel Sauce:
- Drizzle the caramel sauce over the top of the bread pudding, ensuring it's evenly distributed.

Bake:
- Bake in the preheated oven for 45-50 minutes or until the pudding is set and the top is golden brown.

Cool and Serve:
- Allow the bread pudding to cool for a bit before serving. Dust with powdered sugar if desired.

Serve Warm:
- Serve the Apple and Caramel Bread Pudding warm. You can enjoy it on its own or with a scoop of vanilla ice cream.

Enjoy:
- Enjoy the rich, comforting flavors of apple and caramel in this delightful bread pudding!

This Apple and Caramel Bread Pudding is a perfect dessert for fall or any time you crave a warm and indulgent treat. The combination of sweet apples, caramel, and custardy bread makes it a cozy and satisfying dessert.

Apple and Cinnamon Popcorn

Ingredients:

- 1/2 cup popcorn kernels (or pre-popped popcorn)
- 1/4 cup unsalted butter
- 1/4 cup brown sugar
- 1 teaspoon ground cinnamon
- 1/4 teaspoon salt
- 1/2 cup dried apple chips, chopped
- 1/4 cup chopped nuts (such as almonds or pecans), optional

Instructions:

Pop the Popcorn:
- If using popcorn kernels, pop them according to the package instructions. If using pre-popped popcorn, have it ready.

Prepare Add-Ins:
- Chop the dried apple chips and gather the chopped nuts if you're using them.

Make Cinnamon Sugar Coating:
- In a small saucepan, melt the butter over medium heat. Add brown sugar, ground cinnamon, and salt. Stir until the sugar is dissolved, and the mixture is well combined.

Coat the Popcorn:
- Place the popped popcorn in a large bowl. Pour the cinnamon sugar mixture over the popcorn, tossing gently to coat evenly.

Add Dried Apples and Nuts:
- Add the chopped dried apples and nuts to the popcorn mixture. Toss again to distribute them evenly.

Let it Set:
- Allow the coated popcorn to cool and let the cinnamon sugar mixture set, usually for about 10-15 minutes.

Serve:
- Once set, serve the Apple and Cinnamon Popcorn in a bowl or portion it into individual servings.

Enjoy:
- Enjoy this sweet and spiced popcorn as a delicious snack or treat!

This Apple and Cinnamon Popcorn combines the flavors of fall with the sweetness of dried apples and the warmth of cinnamon. It's perfect for movie nights, parties, or simply as a delightful snack to satisfy your sweet cravings.

Apple and Cheddar Soup

Ingredients:

- 2 tablespoons unsalted butter
- 1 onion, diced
- 2 cloves garlic, minced
- 2 large apples, peeled, cored, and chopped (such as Granny Smith)
- 3 cups vegetable or chicken broth
- 3 cups peeled and diced potatoes
- 1 teaspoon dried thyme
- 1 bay leaf
- Salt and black pepper, to taste
- 2 cups sharp cheddar cheese, shredded
- 1 cup whole milk or heavy cream
- Chopped chives or green onions for garnish (optional)

Instructions:

Saute Vegetables:
- In a large pot, melt the butter over medium heat. Add diced onions and cook until they become translucent. Add minced garlic and cook for another 1-2 minutes.

Add Apples and Potatoes:
- Stir in the chopped apples and diced potatoes. Cook for about 5 minutes, allowing them to soften slightly.

Pour in Broth:
- Pour in the vegetable or chicken broth, and add the dried thyme and bay leaf. Season with salt and black pepper to taste. Bring the mixture to a boil, then reduce the heat to low, cover, and simmer until the potatoes are tender.

Blend the Soup:
- Remove the bay leaf, and use an immersion blender to puree the soup until smooth. Alternatively, transfer the soup in batches to a blender, blend, and return it to the pot.

Add Cheese and Milk:
- Stir in the shredded cheddar cheese until melted. Pour in the whole milk or heavy cream, and stir until well combined. Adjust the seasoning as needed.

Simmer:
- Allow the soup to simmer for an additional 5-10 minutes, allowing the flavors to meld.

Serve:
- Ladle the Apple and Cheddar Soup into bowls. Garnish with chopped chives or green onions if desired.

Enjoy:
- Serve this delicious and creamy soup hot, and enjoy the comforting combination of sweet apples and sharp cheddar.

This Apple and Cheddar Soup is a delightful twist on classic potato soup, offering a perfect blend of sweet and savory flavors. It's a wonderful choice for a cozy fall or winter meal.

Apple and Cinnamon Rice Pudding

Ingredients:

- 1 cup Arborio rice
- 4 cups whole milk
- 1/2 cup granulated sugar
- 1 teaspoon ground cinnamon
- 1/4 teaspoon salt
- 1 large apple, peeled, cored, and finely chopped
- 1 teaspoon vanilla extract
- 1/2 cup raisins (optional)
- Ground cinnamon and apple slices for garnish

Instructions:

Rinse Rice:
- Rinse the Arborio rice under cold water until the water runs clear.

Combine Ingredients:
- In a medium-sized saucepan, combine the rinsed rice, whole milk, sugar, ground cinnamon, and salt.

Cook Rice:
- Bring the mixture to a gentle simmer over medium heat, stirring frequently to prevent the rice from sticking to the bottom of the pan.

Add Chopped Apple:
- Once the rice is partially cooked and the mixture has thickened, add the finely chopped apple and continue to simmer until the rice is tender and the pudding reaches your desired consistency.

Optional Raisins:
- If you're using raisins, add them to the rice pudding during the last few minutes of cooking.

Add Vanilla Extract:
- Stir in the vanilla extract for added flavor.

Cool:
- Remove the rice pudding from the heat and let it cool for a few minutes.

Serve:
- Spoon the Apple and Cinnamon Rice Pudding into serving bowls.

Garnish:

- Garnish with a sprinkle of ground cinnamon and slices of fresh apple.

Serve Warm or Chilled:
- Serve the rice pudding warm or chill it in the refrigerator for a few hours before serving.

Enjoy:
- Enjoy the comforting flavors of apple and cinnamon in this delightful rice pudding!

This Apple and Cinnamon Rice Pudding is a comforting and sweet treat, perfect for dessert or even as a cozy breakfast. The combination of creamy rice pudding with the warmth of cinnamon and the sweetness of apples is sure to be a hit!

Apple and Cranberry Stuffed Pork Chops

Ingredients:

- 4 thick-cut boneless pork chops
- Salt and black pepper, to taste
- 1 tablespoon olive oil

For the Stuffing:

- 1 cup finely chopped apples (such as Granny Smith)
- 1/2 cup dried cranberries
- 1/2 cup chopped pecans or walnuts
- 1/4 cup finely chopped onion
- 2 tablespoons butter
- 1 teaspoon dried sage
- Salt and black pepper, to taste

For the Glaze:

- 1/4 cup apple cider or apple juice
- 2 tablespoons maple syrup
- 1 tablespoon Dijon mustard

Instructions:

Preheat Oven:
- Preheat your oven to 375°F (190°C).

Prepare the Stuffing:
- In a skillet, melt butter over medium heat. Add chopped apples, dried cranberries, chopped nuts, finely chopped onion, dried sage, salt, and black pepper. Cook until the apples are softened and the mixture is well combined. Set aside to cool.

Create a Pocket in Pork Chops:
- With a sharp knife, create a pocket in each pork chop by cutting horizontally into the thickest part, being careful not to cut all the way through.

Season and Stuff Pork Chops:
- Season the pork chops with salt and black pepper. Stuff each pocket with the cooled apple and cranberry mixture.

Secure with Toothpicks:
- Use toothpicks to secure the opening of each pork chop, holding the stuffing inside.

Sear Pork Chops:
- In an oven-safe skillet, heat olive oil over medium-high heat. Sear the stuffed pork chops for 2-3 minutes on each side until browned.

Prepare the Glaze:
- In a small bowl, whisk together apple cider or apple juice, maple syrup, and Dijon mustard to create the glaze.

Brush with Glaze:
- Brush the pork chops with the glaze mixture.

Bake in the Oven:
- Transfer the skillet to the preheated oven and bake for about 20-25 minutes or until the pork chops are cooked through.

Baste with Glaze:
- Occasionally, baste the pork chops with the glaze during the baking process to keep them moist.

Rest and Serve:
- Allow the stuffed pork chops to rest for a few minutes before serving.

Enjoy:
- Serve the Apple and Cranberry Stuffed Pork Chops with any remaining glaze drizzled over the top. Enjoy this festive and flavorful dish!

These Apple and Cranberry Stuffed Pork Chops make for a delicious and elegant meal, perfect for special occasions or a cozy family dinner. The combination of savory pork, sweet apples, and tart cranberries creates a delightful balance of flavors.

Apple and Pomegranate Guacamole

Ingredients:

- 3 ripe avocados, peeled, pitted, and mashed
- 1 medium apple, finely diced (such as Granny Smith)
- 1/2 cup pomegranate arils
- 1/4 cup red onion, finely chopped
- 1/4 cup fresh cilantro, chopped
- 1 jalapeño, seeds removed and finely chopped (optional for heat)
- 1-2 cloves garlic, minced
- Juice of 2 limes
- Salt and black pepper, to taste

Instructions:

Prepare Avocados:
- In a bowl, mash the ripe avocados with a fork or potato masher until smooth.

Add Lime Juice:
- Squeeze the juice of 2 limes over the mashed avocados and stir to combine. This not only adds flavor but helps prevent browning.

Mix in Ingredients:
- Gently fold in the finely diced apple, pomegranate arils, chopped red onion, chopped cilantro, chopped jalapeño (if using), and minced garlic.

Season:
- Season the guacamole with salt and black pepper to taste. Adjust the seasoning as needed.

Chill (Optional):
- If time allows, refrigerate the guacamole for about 30 minutes to let the flavors meld. This step is optional but can enhance the overall taste.

Serve:
- Serve the Apple and Pomegranate Guacamole in a bowl.

Garnish (Optional):
- Garnish with extra cilantro, pomegranate arils, or a slice of lime.

Enjoy:
- Enjoy the refreshing and fruity twist to traditional guacamole with the sweetness of apples and the burst of flavor from pomegranate arils!

This Apple and Pomegranate Guacamole is perfect as a snack, appetizer, or a vibrant addition to your Mexican-inspired meals. The combination of creamy avocados, crisp apples, and juicy pomegranate arils creates a delightful and colorful guacamole.

Apple and Cinnamon Rice Krispie Treats

Ingredients:

- 6 cups crispy rice cereal (like Rice Krispies)
- 4 cups mini marshmallows
- 1/4 cup unsalted butter
- 1/2 cup dried apple pieces, chopped
- 1 teaspoon ground cinnamon
- 1/2 teaspoon vanilla extract
- Pinch of salt

Instructions:

Prepare Pan:
- Grease a 9x13-inch baking dish or line it with parchment paper.

Melt Butter:
- In a large pot over medium heat, melt the butter.

Add Marshmallows:
- Add the mini marshmallows to the melted butter and stir continuously until the marshmallows are completely melted and smooth.

Add Cinnamon and Vanilla:
- Stir in the ground cinnamon and vanilla extract, mixing well.

Add Dried Apples:
- Fold in the chopped dried apple pieces, ensuring they are evenly distributed in the marshmallow mixture.

Add Crispy Rice Cereal:
- Remove the pot from heat and gently fold in the crispy rice cereal, making sure to coat the cereal evenly with the marshmallow mixture.

Press into Pan:
- Transfer the mixture to the prepared baking dish. Using a spatula or greased hands, press the mixture firmly and evenly into the pan.

Cool:
- Allow the Apple and Cinnamon Rice Krispie Treats to cool at room temperature until they are set.

Cut into Squares:
- Once set, cut the treats into squares or bars.

Serve:
- Serve and enjoy these delicious Apple and Cinnamon Rice Krispie Treats!

These treats offer a delightful twist to the classic Rice Krispie Treats with the addition of dried apples and warm cinnamon flavor. They are perfect for snacks, lunchboxes, or dessert and bring a taste of autumn to this beloved treat.

Apple and Cheddar Hand Pies

Ingredients:

For the Filling:

- 3 cups apples, peeled, cored, and diced (such as Granny Smith)
- 1/4 cup granulated sugar
- 1/4 cup brown sugar
- 1 teaspoon ground cinnamon
- 1/4 teaspoon ground nutmeg
- 1 tablespoon lemon juice
- 1 tablespoon all-purpose flour
- 1 cup sharp cheddar cheese, shredded

For the Pie Crust:

- 2 1/2 cups all-purpose flour
- 1 cup unsalted butter, cold and cubed
- 1 teaspoon salt
- 1 teaspoon granulated sugar
- 1/4 to 1/2 cup ice water

For Assembly:

- 1 egg (for egg wash)
- Additional granulated sugar (for sprinkling)

Instructions:

For the Pie Crust:

Prepare Ingredients:
- Cut the cold butter into small cubes.

Combine Dry Ingredients:
- In a large bowl, combine the all-purpose flour, salt, and granulated sugar.

Incorporate Butter:
- Add the cold, cubed butter to the flour mixture. Use a pastry cutter or your fingers to work the butter into the flour until it resembles coarse crumbs.

Add Ice Water:

- Gradually add ice water, 1 tablespoon at a time, and mix until the dough just comes together. Be careful not to overmix.

Form Dough:
- Divide the dough in half, form each half into a disc, wrap in plastic wrap, and refrigerate for at least 1 hour.

For the Filling:

Preheat Oven:
- Preheat your oven to 375°F (190°C).

Prepare Filling:
- In a bowl, combine diced apples, granulated sugar, brown sugar, ground cinnamon, ground nutmeg, lemon juice, and all-purpose flour. Mix well. Fold in the shredded cheddar cheese.

Assembly:

Roll Out Dough:
- Roll out each disc of chilled dough on a floured surface to about 1/8-inch thickness.

Cut Out Rounds:
- Using a round cutter or a bowl as a guide, cut out rounds of dough.

Add Filling:
- Place a spoonful of the apple and cheddar filling in the center of each round.

Seal and Crimp Edges:
- Fold the dough over the filling to create a half-moon shape. Use a fork to crimp and seal the edges.

Brush with Egg Wash:
- Beat the egg and brush it over the tops of the hand pies for a golden finish.

Sprinkle with Sugar:
- Sprinkle a little granulated sugar over the tops of the hand pies.

Bake:
- Place the hand pies on a baking sheet and bake in the preheated oven for about 20-25 minutes, or until the crust is golden brown.

Cool and Serve:
- Allow the Apple and Cheddar Hand Pies to cool slightly before serving. Enjoy!

These Apple and Cheddar Hand Pies combine the sweet and savory flavors of apple and cheese in a portable and delightful treat. They are perfect for sna

Printed in the USA
CPSIA information can be obtained
at www.ICGtesting.com
LVHW082037010624
781791LV00010B/181